Angletwitch and Poppydocks

A collection of Cornish Dialect words and stories

Edited by
George Pritchard

Federation of Old Cornwall Societies

ISBN 978-0-902660-41-0

Published by
The Federation of Old Cornwall Societies
"Wingfield" 5, British Road
St Agnes, Cornwall, TR5 0TX

www.oldcornwall.org

© Federation of Old Cornwall Societies, 2010

All rights reserved.
No reproduction permitted without the prior
permission of the publisher.

PREFACE

Ninety years ago, a group of people met in St Ives Cornwall to listen to a talk on the local dialect, from this meeting came the formation of the first Old Cornwall Society and a movement that has now grown to 46 individual Societies throughout Cornwall. The Societies work together under the auspices of the Federation to collect and protect all things Cornish.

All those years ago people were worried about the decline in the use of dialect words. However, when two or three Cornish people get together the accents are strong and the use of some dialect is heard with its individual sounds of vowel and consonant and the very special way these are woven to form sentences.

When I was growing up, dialect was then the most natural way of speech amongst the older generation and the first word I remember asking about was when my grandmother would say to me, "wus matter wi?". 'Wi', I was told by my mother, meant 'with you'.

Sayings and similies were duly instilled in me and when my mother had her wool in a 'dole' Father would say, "It's a tangled spellar", a fishing term, such as were used a great deal then.

At school children were discouraged from using dialect as it was felt that it would threaten their job prospects in the future. However, when I started work as a mason's apprentice the dialect just flowed from the men with whom I worked.

Towsers - crouse - crib - mazed Monday - 'ellens - short stone - yanks -skew - skud - dag - showel - gad -etc., etc. These words became a fascination and I started to collect them. Thankfully, I was not alone and people in other parts of Cornwall gathered up words with their meanings and saved them from being lost forever.

The local radio also played its part with recordings being made which allow us to hear how different dialect words were used to describe an object. With the help of those who made the recordings we are placing some on our web site (http://cornishdialect.oldcornwall.org).

2010 is the ninetieth anniversary of that first Old Cornwall group. In the years that have followed, thousands of words and their meanings have been collected, along with sayings and phrases. The aim of the web site is to make the collection available to people in Cornwall and around the world, and we hope that those who are the descendents of Cornish emigrants will let us know if they find words that are still in use by their families and communities. I would like to thank my predecessor Joy Stephenson and all those others whose dedication has made the production of this book possible.

I must also thank the Cornish Gorsedd which through its competitions has stimulated the writing of dialect prose and verse pieces over the years and this booklet contains pieces selected from those awarded prizes.

Brian Stevens, Federation Dialect Recorder

VERY OLD PECULIAR SAYINGS FROM ST. IVES

Off wi': Be off with you!

Go thou wust home: Go on your way home.

Larruping: Blowing idly in the wind as a ship's sail. Dragging in the mud.

Galere: Pronounced gal-ee-er. Suspect Breton origin. A predicament or state of distress.

Rub-a-dull-ion: A loud noise, people shouting or quarrelling.

Thee'st like Jackie Broad's basin in two parts: The story goes that Jackie Broad's basin was a cherished one. He lent it to a neighbour and it was returned, broken, in two parts. This saying originated from my paternal grandfather, born about 1825, in St. Ives, and was used a lot at that time.

Thee'st like Johnnie Hat and Mary Ann Polka: They never went to bed the same day as they got up. A happy couple whose only interest was to enjoy themselves and with no cares for work. This is a lovely one. Who was Johnnie Hat? Who was Mary Ann Polka? They were real people. These were their nick-names. What a pity there is no authoritative record. All sorts of situations could be imagined. This was a much quoted saying heard in my youth about folk who kept late hours.

Thy tongue is going like a lillybanger: What is a lillybanger? Describes ceaseless talk about nothing in particular.

As light as a piece of Jane Warren's heavy cake: Jane Warren lived in a small house on Victoria Hill, half way down on left hand side. Every week she made heavy cake and my father, as a young boy, craftily hung around when the cake baking day came, and he usually was given a slice. He was born in 1860 so this would have been circa 1870 or near.

Wash trough or troy: A wooden sort of cradle shaped box, approx. one yard long, 18in. high, 18in. wide. The women washed their clothes in same. About 1880-1900.

Thee'st like Old Worm's fool: Old Worm's fool was a simple man who used to assist in smuggling around 1840-1850. Who was he? When Custom men questioned him, he was taught to reply: "I don't knaw," and this was his reply to all awkward questions.

As big as Mary Booshee: Who was Mary Booshee? My father said she was the biggest woman ever known in St. Ives, and to be told you were like her was a great insult.

As big a liar as Tom Pepper: I do not think this is particularly south west Cornwall, although I have only heard westcountry people use it.

You can't have it in hake and herring too: Same as 'the ha'penny and the bun' - not both ways.

A gurry load: A load of anything, full and running over. It's a recognised weight of fish.

Poor sawl went off in a decline: Some one died of tuberculosis.

Puggy's calf: Pronounced Pug gee, meaning the very stupidest person ever. To be told you have no more sense than Puggy's calf means you are of the lowest intelligence possible.

Old Luke's ducks: Thee'st like old Luke's ducks, never go further by day than they can return home by nightfall.

Old Troon's bus: Bus ran between St. Ives and Penzance, must be at least 90 - 100 years ago. When an overcrowded bus or train came along, my father would remark: This is like old Troon's bus always room for one more.

Old smugglers make the best Customs men: Obvious meaning, they know all the tricks and evasions.

Maffo's old donkey: Probably means Matthew's old donkey. An old donkey which used to drag up the Stennack from the town, stopping at every door for tit-bits. Anyone late home was said to be "like Maffo's old donkey", late and long overdue.

Jane (Edwards) Hynd

First published in Old Cornwall, Vol.VIII, No.5.

-o-

A Mine of Information.

A long time ago when a rail journey to London was an adventure, a Cornish miner and his son made the trip and spent most of the time in seeing the sights.

Gazing at Buckingham Palace the boy asked, "Wha's that Da?" "Don't knaw, son."

The same question at the Horse Guards, the Houses of Parliament and elsewhere produced equally uninforming replies.

"Doan't mind me asking questions do 'ee, Da?" "Naw," was the answer, "if 'ee niver ask no questions thee'll niver larn nawthen."

First published in Old Cornwall, Vol. VI, No. 6.

-o-

Likes

Portraying a tall, thin person – "like a yard of pump water."

Describing a female whose hair is tightly drawn back from the forehead – or in these days – the possessor of an Eton crop – "like a scraaped cunger."

First published in Old Cornwall, Vol. 1, No. 9.

MY GOOD FRIDAY'S OUTEN

By 'JAN'

When I wor going up the road Good Friday forenoon, thinks I, "Why, Jan, thee'st knaw the auld pig es for the market nixt waik, and thee'st ought be looking out fur a young sucker to take the place of 'n; thee'st better make 'quiries of the fust keenly man thee'st mait"; so when I got up to the village and there was old Dicky Chenawden who b'long worken down along with Squire Tucker, "Here," sez I, "thee'rt the very wan I want for ta see, dost tha knaw anywan what 'a got some young suckers for sale?"

"Iss," sez ee, "old Farmer 'Vaskis over to 'Varth 'e got a fine lot of veers, but I da b'laive he want for to sell the old sow along with 'em."

"Aw," sez I, "I d' only want wan sucker, now tis coming in summer, I only b'long keep two in tha winter—bit company like in the dark nights, an' 'elp keep wan tother warm, thee'st knaw."

"Lev me see," sez Dicky, "why I belaive Farmer Jinkin, up Pennance, ought t' 'ave a belly of veers about now; thee'st better go up and see 'e 'bout it." So off I goes, soase, up to Pennance and see'd Farmer Jinkin, and sure 'nough 'e had as fine a belly of veers as one wud wish for ta see, and I 'greed 'long weth un to come up fur wan, ind nixt waik.

Well, soase, what I were wanten tell 'ee was, that when I comed out of Farmer Jenkin's, I seed heaps of men, wemmen and cheldern carren baskets and kittles, and the little maids 'ad fiam new dolls carryen, goen all in some coose up a lane laiden to Carn Marth, — "What's up?" sez I to myself, "I belaive I'd best folly 'em and see what they be apon, t'day's Good Friday, too, and I arn't working afore 'morrow marning, so I'd as well make a day of it now I'm here?" Well, I folleyed 'em for bout a quarter mile, s'pose, when they put down their baskets and kittles on the ground. The wemmen and some of the men sot down, too, but all the young cheldern runned away down out o' sight, so I stanked out as fast as I cud to see where they was going to, and when I got there, they was all down by a will.

"What will es this?" sez I. "I dedn' knaw there was narry wan here!" and they all said, a'most in wan breth "This is Figgie Dowdy's Will, maister!"

"Figgie Dowdy?" sez I. "Why. I never 'eard tell of no sech man, nor wumman neither!" "You 'aven'," sez a ould man weth grey wiskers up to un, who they called Mester Treloar, "Well, I s'pose I be the ouldest wan 'bout here and I cain't mind th' ould fella, mesilf, but I've allers ben tould as 'ow 'e lived 'ere 'bouts and maade this here will fur isself, an' by raison other people comed 'ere and tooked away a's water, 'e put a door pon the will and locken'd up so they shudn'.—Come'st down 'ere, and see where 'e had a's hangens to, and all." So, soase, I clembed down ovar the bank and there a wor, sure 'nough—two ould crooks 'pon wan side and some ould hits o' iron 'pon tother.

When I'd done looken at un, Mester T'loar asked me ded I iver 'ear tha ould song bout Figgie Dowdy's Will. "Naw," sez I, "I cudn' say as how I ded." So 'e tould off a varse like this here:—

> "Figgie Dowdy 'ad a will,
> Up 'pon top of Carn Marth 'ill,
> He locken'd up by night and day,
> For fear they'd carr' the water 'way."

They do say there wor moor varses, 'bout figs as well as water, an' better po'try too, I shudn' be frightened, but they're all lost and forgotten.

I wor jist upon goin' agin, when a cheeld there bro't her doll up to me, and sez she, "Will 'ee cressen my doll for me, plaise, maister?" "Cresten yer doll, cheeld vean," sez I. "Why, I niver knawed sich things was iver done, and besides, I beant a menister, ef they was!" And then it come to me like a draim, how I'd heard me ould mother say as how she b'longed to 'ave her doll cressened up to Rabbit Rock on Good Fridays—right up 'bove Tank there where "Miner" and "Spitfire" da take in their water to—and 'ere it was, gooin on, and a brave ould conformence it wor, too. Fust the youngest cheeld corned up to Mester T'loar and gove'n her doll, and 'ee axed her what she want'n called. "I da want for 'er to be called Meery," she sez, "'cause my taycher down school towld me a some nice story 'bout Meery last Sunday and I thoft I'd like for me doll to be cressend en Meery, after she." "So she shall, me dear," sez Mester T'loar; "so she shall!" and he bint down to the water and dipped a's 'ands en et, splashed a drap or two ovar the doll's face and eyes and told off "Meery 'ad a little lamb," or something, and sez, "I cressen tha 'Meery!' and then 'e gove'n back to the cheeld agin, and she runned off t'er mawther with her Meery in her arms. So the conformence went on, and me helpen, till they was all cressend, by all such names as "Victoria," and "Martha," and "Flourance," and more'n I can tell, besides.

Well, soase, after the cressenen war ovar thay all filled thar kittles with water from the will, and sez I, "Off home, I s'pose, now 'en, you?" "No," sez thay, "We're goen up Sunny Bank now t'ave our tay, comest 'long weth we, you, and 'ave a dish of tay, too!"

"Thankey, sure," sez I, "It be ter'ble kind of 'ee and I'll be ever sa plaised to 'ave tay 'long weth ee." So off we traipsed till, 'most on top o' Carn Marth, sez Mester T'loar "Now 'ere we are, up ta Sunny Bank, lev us setty down 'ere in the Tooth and 'ave all the sunshine to ourselves, you cheldern be off and get some brouse for the fire, we men'll make a fireplace while tha wemmen da cut up saffern caakes and spread tha bread and butter."

Well, soase, after tay – an' a fine tay, too - we talked some 'bout one thing and some 'bout tother, and somebody sez, "What a lovely view et es, weth Falmouth 'Arbour and all the ships en et!"

"The tide es en," sez another, "for you can see the water up to Devoran."

"It is", sez I, "an you can see most all the Devoran tramline, too, looking fram down below Croft'andy, right up through C'rarrack, along Pennance; way up ta Buller Hill, and part way in 'Druth!"

"Do you knaw," sez a man—I da furgit a's name—"that twas my father cut most of thay moorstone blocks what the rails are fixed pon?"

"No," sez I. "I diden knaw et, you, but 'e must 'a had some big job cutten all they."

"Iss, aw ded," sez tha man, "an I've 'eard en tell as how when aw comed up 'ere from down South Country for ta live, most a 'undred years ago now, Carn Marth wor covered all awver with great moorstone rocks jist like Carn Brea ovar there, but the Devoran Railway wor then maken an' seein' they offered a shellen a piece for any moorstone the right size, took down on the line to em, my father, mother and older brothers turned to, and with boryers, jumpers, feathers and pins and gunpowder they cleared all the rocks off tha top of this place." "Well, now!" sez I "I allers wandered how Carn Brea was covered with sich great stoanes and Carn Marth so bare as a bald 'ead, now I da know why 'tis! Who'd 'a thoft it?"

"An what 'bout thay barrows—tumblers[1] what they da call—that was on top of this hill?" axed anawther man – Thee'st knaw un; ould Jack Trewin—"I 'eard the schoolmaister up to St. Dye say as how there wore three tumblers here weth ould Ancient British Kings burrid en em till some miners scat em up, more'n a hundred years ago, looking for treasure. When they got ta the middle of 'em they found nawthen but some ould cloamen pots fulled up with ashes, and they was sa mazed 'bout et that they thrawed em on the floor and scat em all to sherds."

"Aw! cloamen pots?—What a pity," sez I, "They might 'a maade 'andsome orneymints for somewan's dresser or mantlepiece!" We stopped thar chatting 'bout wan thing and tother all about Carn Marth till the sun wor going down, so 'Sunny Bank' wadn' sunny no moor and a wor time for we all to git off home agin, arid when I got down to the village who do 'ee think I seed agin but Dicky Chenawden comen out of the 'Siven Stars'.

"Well," sez 'e "ave 'ee bot yer young sucker?"

---

[1] The Ordnance Survey shows three tumuli on the hill.

"'Iss, I've been an' spoke for un," sez I, "and I be mighty well plaised with the looks of un."

"I'm glad for to 'ear et'"', sez Dicky, "and I da wesh 'ee tha best of luck weth un when you do git un."

"Thankey" sez I, "I've 'ad luck by un already, for—my lor—what weth Figgie Dowdy's Will, and tumblers weth cloamen pots, an' all, I shain't fergit this Good Friday for 'ears to come. I niver knawed so much 'bout Carn Marth afore, and I shudn knaw et now ef I dedn' go see for that young sucker up ta Farmer Jinkin's."

First published in Old Cornwall, Vol. I, No.12.

-o-

Helpful

"Well, Mr. Pascoe, what's your trouble?" asked a young doctor from up-country, taking his first surgery in a Cornish village.

"Cain't clunky."

(*"Collenky, cowl lenky,* vb., to swallow down: as *lenky, later clonca, klunka..."* Cornish English Dicionary).

Cold comfort on the Farm.

When a village shopkeeper commented on the small size of the eggs offered, the wholesaler said "They edn' thrawin no bigs uns this cold weather."

Dogmatical

Two Cornish women were discussing the identity of a stranger who had been seen in the village.

"E's a passon, you," said one, "I seen 'im weth 'is collar back to forth."

First published in Old Cornwall, Vol. VII, pages 286, 401 & 410.

Fore Street, Bodmin, c.1910

THE SUMMONS

By Beryl West

*(Awarded first prize and the Rosemergy Cup
in the 1973 Gorsedd Competition)*

    'Ave 'ee ever 'ad won of thai theer summonses? You da naw, to attend Crown Court at Bodmin?

    I da remember me Feerther 'ad won wonce: twud 'ave bin round ninetain thirty I s'ppose, 'for last war anyway. Course twaden Crown Court thin, 'twas Bodmin Assizes.

    But 'eer let me tell 'ee the plod.

    I da remember 'twas a day en early Mai I found me Mawther waatin' fer me outside our front duhr en Saaint Ives wen I cum 'ome fer me dener from shop.

    "Look, Dorcas, what's cum fer yeer Feerther", shai sed waivin' a geet honvelope en front of me wid 'On His Majesty's Service' bawldly prented across en.

    "What es a?"

"Ow shud I naw! But I don' like the look ob en - I wish yeer Feerther wud 'urry up an' cum 'ome en open en. That awld sly boots Dick Staivens the postman sed 'twas a summons!" Mawther wuz en sum state sure nuff shai aiven scat the clome to shurds en the bawl on the kechen taible wid excitement an' thin burnt the stoo, so we 'ad to maike do wid a jamie maw fer our dener.

The honvelope wuz put on the shilf above the owld slab wheer everywon cud sai en as soon as thai entered the kechen, 'cos the slab wuz Mawther's pride an' joy shai kept en shinin', alwais rubben en up wid black lead an' Brasso!

Well, Feerther caime 'ome tai time, mackerl danglin' from es fengers so I nawd thin wai'd 'ave sumtheng to ait.

"Mathey, look!" sed Mawther, waivin' the honvelope en front ob en fer 'ee cud put es foot en the kechen.

Feerther opened en quick like.

"I got to go to Bodmin Assizes, Mawther, on twenty fefth Jooly of 'ee plaise!" 'ee sed, proper mazed but lookin' cauld as a quilkin wid fright. Nivver Mathey! 'Ow can 'ee? Thee'll be out feshen!"

But 'twas me oncle Paiter 'oo told Feerther wat to do.

"Go an' see auld Doctor Price" 'ee sed, "I 'ad won an' 'ee gob me a letter to send 'em. I nivver went! Thee don' want to go up theer, Mathey! That theer murder caise is commn' up you d'naw—the boy 'oo murdered es feerther and mawther. You go an' see awid Doctor Price, take that theer Summons wid 'ee"

Feerther cuden git to the surgery quick enough; 'ee wuz furst in the queue of panel pashents that aivenen.

"Well, Mathey," sed Doctor Price 'oo'd bin the family doctor fer years, "What can I do fer 'ee?"

"Tco thoo 'oor Summons, Doctor. Paiter sed I shud cum an' see 'ee 'cos thees 'ed gob me a letter fer the Court."

Doctor Price shook 'es 'ead. "Sorry Mathey, nawthen doin'. I cain't 'elp 'ee. Paiter 'ad shengles wen I gob 'ee a letter. Gus on wid 'ee Mathey, thee'll enjoy yerself. I 'spect et'll be that theer murder caise— you da naw, the boy ''oo murdered es feerther an' mawther."

Feerther cudden wait to 'eer no more; desappointed 'ee left the surgery, but a couple of days afterwards Feerther saw Sergint Bennets, won of the local policemen an' mentioned the summons to 'ee.

"Well, Mathey, I reckon thee'll 'ave to go. Only doctor can get 'ee off that theer summons," sed the Sergint graively.

"Iss, I da naw. I've bin to see en an' 'ee won't gob me no letter," sed Feerther sadly.

"Well ,Mathey, everyman must do 'es dooty. I 'spect thees'll be on that theer murder caise—you da naw, the boy 'oo murdered 'es feerther an' mawther ..."

But Feerther deden wait fer en to finish, 'ee wuz already 'alf way 'ome.

But like all thengs gradually the twenty-fefth Jooly caime. Et wuz a Toosday an' Feerther'd arranged to go up to Bodmin on the seben o'clock train en the mornin'.

On the Monday, after doin' the waik's washen, Mawther wuz cookin' all day. 'Tween teers an' sobs shai baiked a pasty, saffern caike wid rate butter an' aiven 'eavy caike which shai took down to Jan Staivens baik 'awse to cook fer Feerther's crowst. Now Bodmin es forty-five miles awai from Saaint Ives an' Feerther 'ad nivver bin feerther thin Penzance en es life.

En the aivenen all the family arrived to see Feerther, won by won, furst Oncle Paiter, en second-best suit, sadly shaiken es 'ead; then Feerther's sester. Aunt Tillie, all 'cited like, squawken like a 'en an' gittin' Feerther so worked up 'ee wuz scattin' baccy all over the ketchen floor; thin the Vecar caime to wish en well (Mawther got out the best clome for 'ee); aiven Gramma caime, magestic en black shawl 'an waiven 'er ditty bag en front of everywon; shai wuz nearly ninetai but strong as a hoss!

'Twas a breer crant!

Thai ait a gurry load of saffern caike an' drank tai by the gallon, but I cud see Feerther keepin' an eye on the pasty - after all Bodmin wuz a breer wal an' 'ee 'ad to 'ave sumthen to ait fer crowst.

But by eleven everywon 'ad gone an wai all wint to bed, though wai deden 'spect to slaip much that night.

But we must 'ave dropped off 'cos nixt theng I nawd wuz bein' woken up wid a bang begger than a clap o' thunder.

I slipt wid me sester Honor an' shai shot out of the bed.

"Tes the lifebaw rocket, Dorcas," she screeched.

Just thin the sky lit up as the second rocket went up an' theer wuz another terrible bang.

Now Feerther wuz a member of the lifebaw crew an' within seconds 'ee wuz downsteers almost 'fore me an Honor 'ad lit our candle.

"Better dress an' go down to the 'arbour an' see wat est all 'bout", sed Mawther goin' downsteers wid 'er candle to put the kittle on.

We were all fengers an' thumbs an' we were en such a 'urry we deden aiven stop to comb our 'ull or wash our chacks. Twaden a rough night but the wind 'ad got up a bit an' 'twas a guts of raain.

Mawther put the kittle on the gas reng though twas only thrai o'clock, an' me an' Honor rushed out en the emptin rain to the 'arbour.

Wen me an' Honor got theer the tractor wuz just putten the lifebaw down the slepway ento the waiter; 'twas 'igh waiter an' that maaide the launch aisier, otherwise et wud 'ave to be pulled across the 'arbour sand to the sai. We matched en saail round the Island out of sight.

On the way 'ome we were tawld a saailor 'ad bin taiken ill on board es ship off Gurnards Head 'an the lifebaw wuz taiken Doctor Price out to en, so et wuden likely to be out fer long.

We went back 'ome to Mawther; twas after fawr by thin so we deden bother to undress - we jist laaid on our beds till the alarm went off at ocx.

Wen I went downsteers Mawther stirred as I put the kittle back on the gas reng; "Wat time es et?" shai asked. I told 'er.

"Es yer Feerther back yit?"

"No, not yit! I'll see to es crowst, Mawther," I sed taiken the pasty, heavy caike an' saffern caike from the dresser an' wrappin' them en a clain, awld red 'ankercheef, fer en to taike wi en.

16

Mawther got the fryin' pan out cos shai thaut that goin' all thai miles Feerther shud 'ave a good meal en en. But half past sex caime; thin quarter to seben; thin seben o'clock —an' no Feerther!

"'Ee won't 'ave time to ait nawthen," fretted Mawther, eyein' the clock.

"Nivver mind, I'll gob en a bit more caike to ait on the train," I sed cuttin' the caike agin.

By this time our nixt door neighbour, Maggie Will-Knaw, 'ad arrived. "Wheer's Mathey? Still out wid the lifebaw? My! 'ees gon an' bin an' missed the traain. Wat'll ee do?" shai screeched all en won breath, 'er thert eye twitchin'!

"Leben alone. 'Ow shud I naw? Aben 'ee got no work to do, Maggie?" retorted Mawther, wipin' 'er 'ands on 'er tawser.

By 'alf past seben me Oncle Paiter arrived, sweatin' leakin' from runnun' to sai the bawt wuz just commn' en to the 'arbour. Doctor Price cuden do nawthen fer the saailor oo wuz being taiken to Penzans 'ospital.

Wen Feerther venshully caime en 'ee deden seem too upset till 'ee looked at the clock.

Thin 'ee scratched 'es nuddock. "I've gone an' bin an' missed the traain, Martha," 'ee sed.

"Iss thou art euchred now Mathey," sad Mawther hopelessly.

But Feerther wuz drenken a dish of tai, all thauts of Bodmin far awai from en.

"I'll git Sergint Bennets," sed Oncle Paiter wonce more rushin' out of the 'awse.

Well, Oncle Paiter fetched the sergint an' 'ee scratched es nuddock an' sed Feerther wud still 'ave to go to Bodmin. So Feerther chainged ento es best suit, cursing all the time, an' maaide es way to the station to catch the nixt traain.

Me an' Honor went wid en to carry es crowst for en. But on the way, as we were goin' up Tregenna 'Ill we saw awld Charlie Osborne, a farmer from out Trevalgan wai, commn' down Gabriel Strait en es new car, a geet grai 'Umber; Charlie wuz sum well-to-do farmer!

"Wheer are 'ee goin' all best chainged, Mathey?" shouted Charlie, braiken' by the Passmore Edwards Institute an' frightenin' Feerther 'alf out es wits.

"Bodmin but I've bin an' missed the traain. I'm on the Jury!" sed Feerther, steppin' back quick like on to the paivement. "Got a new car 'ave 'ee Charlie?"

"Iss, only 'ad en a waik. Bodmin? Well 'op in. Twill do 'er good to 'ave a long trip 'an tis market dai en Liskeard. 'Eer, I'll taike 'ee up!"

Now I saw Feerther 'esitate like. Honor an' me nivver thought about et but Charlie Osborne 'ad nivver driven a car fore en es life; but Sergint Bennets wuz soon on the scene an' 'ee tawld Feerther to 'op in an' taike 'vantage of the kind offer. So Feerther reluctantly go en, crowst an' all, an' Charlie drove es geet 'Umber 'ard a starboard an' gob 'er plenty of shait up Tregenna 'Ill an' out of sight.

We nawd Feerther cuden be back early that night but all the family gathered at our 'awse by seben o'clock; Oncle Paiter, Gramma an' two or trai of Feerther's frens; thai were theer drenkin' tai an' 'arbie 'bout aight but 'ee wuz lookin' brebham wished sure nuff; white as death 'ee wuz.

"I've 'ad sum dai! That theer Charlie Osborne eden fitty: 'ee eden saife to be on the roads. 'Ee caint drive that theer geet theng. I wuz sick all the way up fore we left Connor Downs, I wuz, an' by the time we got to Bodmin after 'avin' a puncture on the Moor I cud 'ardly stand. Got a lift to the Court 'awse en a donkey an' shai. I shigged en on the wai 'ome an' cum back by traain." Feerther grabbed a desh of tai; 'ee wuz en sum kilter sure nuff.

"Wat 'appened at the Court then?" asked Mawther, loosenin' Feerther's tie.

"Oh, I'm on the Jury alright, Martha. An' 'tis that theer murder caise. I've got to go up agin tomorra so set the alarm! Course I caint discuss the caise."

"Wat caint 'ee discuss?" screeched Maggie Will-naw, 'oo'd seen Feerther cum so now shai wanted to naw the news; but venshually Mawther got everywon out of the 'awse an' Feerther en bed.

Anyway, Feerther 'ad to go to Bodmin fer thrai wa·iks on that theer triall, thrai walks of traipsin' to an' from an' scrawin' round Bodmin. Feerther 'ad nivver travelled so far or so much en es life befer or after es jury service!

But as 'ee sed afterwards et brought out the best of everywon; all thai twilve jurors wuz afraid thai might do an injustice 'an thai wuz brebham cawshus.

Course, today we don't 'ave to worry bout 'angin' anywon, but we do 'ave to worry bout taiken theer freedom from em, so to spaike; aiven so 'tis a job no won seems to want to do; but as Feerther sed all thai yeers ago, "Somewon must do et!"

First published in Old Cornwall Vol. VIII, No. 4.

-o-

Kayling at St Merryn

SOME SAYINGS IN OUR COMMUNITY

St Gennys

Bag like a bucket. Described a good dairy cow.

Blaw as a niddle. Said of someone who was cold. Blaw = Blue, Niddle = Needle.

Comfortable as an old shoe. Applied to an easygoing person.

Face as long as this week and next. Said of someone who was miserable.

Gruffing and grunting like a boar pig. Said of a pompous old autocrat.

He got a churn of milk from two steers and a lease (dry) **cow**. Said of a person who tended to exaggerate.

He id'n just zackly. Said of someone who is ill.

No more need than a toad needs side pockets. Said of an extravagant demand.

S/he's a gatepost child. Said of a child born out of wedlock.

S/he's got a belly like a Wilkie. Fat as a frog.

Sleep like a ringer. Presumably like a campanologist during sermon time.

So that's what's the matter with Annie's wooden leg. Said when a mystery had been solved. I have no idea who Annie was, or what ailment afflicted her leg.

Sore like a rig. A rig is a large cattle sore.

Recollected by Frank Smeeth as being used in the 1940's.

CORNISH KETCHEN

Ralph Dunstan writes that the traditional tune is found throughout England, but gives no clues as to his source. The Dialect has the usual features of <e> for <i> and as well as much Dialect vocabulary; baal, kiddleewenk, braav etc. The song has Bizza for Bissoe showing the Dialect <o, ow> changing to unstressed <a>. For the tune

and a glossary of the words plus other Cornish Dialect songs go to the web site of the Federation's Folksong and Music Recorder Merv Davey:
http://www.an-daras.com/music/m_dialect.htm

Aw! cum an I'll tell ee a taal,
A taal o tha days ov oald,
Bowt Aadum Tregay an es wife
Oo livd up ta Bizza I'm toald.

Sengen too-raa-laa loo-raa – loo
Ri too-raa-laa loo-raa-lay
Too-raa-laa loo-raa-loo
Ri too-raa-laa loo-raa –lay

Aadum woz fond ov es drop,
A bowzer woz nawthen ta ee
Wen ee awt ta be up ta tha baal
Ee wud rether be aven a spree

Wawn Saterdae nite az I've eeard,
Ee went ta tha kidleewenk
An wot weth tha beer an tha'et
Ee soon woz too droozled ta thenk.

Goyn oamloang, be shur ee got maazd,
Ee dedn naw weer ee woz to:
Ez ed like a wezz-a-bowt turnd,
An a cudn tell wot a shud doo.

Twoz raenen an blawen braav an aard
An ee creedeld aloang like-a-theng
Till at laas ee faald down en a adet
An et ez oald ed weth a deng!

Oald Jinee woz oam waeten fer un
An claenen hup oll tha cloam
But soon she got tyrd ov thaat,
An sit owt ta breng un oam.

An az she went traapsen aloang,
She thot thaat she eeard un screech
"Weer ar ee, oal maan?" sez she
"Yooom saem en a purdee smeech!"

"Aw! Jinee, I'm ded," sez ee,
"Me mowth-saych ez oll gawn!"

"Theert a lyard, I'm shoor," sez she
"A droozen ed sellee oald zawn!"

She got un rite owt at lass,
An tuk un saaf oam ta bed
An gibm a baasun a broath,
An plaesterd ez broakun ed.

Nex mornen she appd ta geek
Owt onder tha wina bline
An theer woz tha Passun owtside
Oll dissd hup braav an fine.

 "Aw! git en tha spens," sez she,
"Aw! git en an eed awae:
Ef Passun shud see ee like this,
Wotiver wud a sae?

Tha Passun ee soon begend
Sum Screptur ta recoall
"Good wummun," sez ee, "I spoas
Yoov eeard ov Aadum's Foall?"

"Shed jist thenk I av," sez she,
An then ta Aadum ded coall
"Come owt from en onder tha spens,
Fur tha Passun da naw et aoll!

SOME SAYINGS IN OUR COMMUNITY

Padstow

As soft as a Wollop. Very easy going.

Black from naws to claws. Dirty all over.

I'm Braben Whisht. I'm feeling poorly.

Comeretowance. Come here at once.
Eppy as a wheelbarrow. Eccentric.
Flam new. Brand new.
Gain like a lone dog. Rushing about.
Ghastly Toad. Nasty person.
Gidon withee. Stop teasing.
Gidd alone do. Would you believe it?
He'd fight is awn shada. Aggressive.
I could sleep on a clthes line. Very tired.
I'm up to me eyes in daisies. Very busy.
I'ts a bit zam zaudly. Cool or tasteless.
It melts in your mouth like Hoss Shoe Nails. Used to describe food that is hard or tough.
Knaw nothing. Said of a person who is stupid.
Leathered Black and Blue. Thrashed.
Limp as a dish rag. Sagging.
Maazed as a Brush. Eccentric or annoyed
Maaking me hade addled. Confused.
Naaked as a Jay Bird. Nude.
Orright ar ee? Are you well?
Proper Job. Well done.
Scat un down. Knock him/ it down.
She's like an old hen. Fussy.
Skate Mouth. Loud mouth, loose tongued.
Squall [to]. To cry.
Stop frecking around. Stop wasting time.
Stubborn as a waggon 'oss. Stubborn.
Taisey as a snake. S/he's irritable.
Tedden Zackly. Not quite right.

Tedden that toal. I made a mistake

The meat is pindy. Gone off.

With thanks to members of the Padstow Old Cornwall Society

-o-

A DECOCTION OF BROOM.

A re-told story by William Bottrell

A few years since, a gentleman from a distant part of the country, who went to reside in St. Levan, almost daily visited Pergwarra, and passed some time in gossiping with a primitive old couple who lived in a cottage close by the cove.

One day he found the old man sitting in the chimney-corner, groaning very much. To enquiries as to what was the matter, the old man replied, "I'm very bad weth a creck en my cheens. I caen't hardly stand nor set, and I cudn' travel to saave my life; I wesh you cud tell me what wed do me any good. Meary theer wed have me lay 'pon the flure weth my faace down, that she may stank an' jump on my back—she well have et tha's the best cure for a crick, 'an es some vexed 'cause I waent laive her to. Ef I cud toss her off my back an' break her neck, she might try her jumpen!"

"Ef I cud have my well on thee, Josey," said the old woman, "I'd put thee en a wheel-barra an' trundle thee out 'pon the Haw; thee west git up an' come in again fast 'nough, I'll be bound. But I wesh, Sir, after that, that you cud tell what wed do'n any good, for there he've ben, this two-three days, stuck 'pon the chimbley-stool all the blessed day so cross as a peg. One caen't vinture to spaik for'n!"

"Well, if he has the lumbago," the gentleman said "I believe that a strong decoction of green broom is as good a remedy for it as anything you can get from the doctor."

"O tell me, Sir, how I can maake the somethen 'nuther you're tellen of weth grane broom, an' I'll set about et to wonst," said An Mary, "for I'll do anythen in life to git Josey out of the house again!"

The visitor explained what a decoction was. "Just boil broom, the stuff you make brooms of," said he; and directly he left An Mary went off and soon returned with an armful of the plant which she thought to be recommended, boiled it a few hours, strained the decoction, got her good man to bed, bathed his back and bound a good bunch of the herbs on to the aching cheens.

Next morning the gentleman called to know if his prescription was having the desired effect; "I hope you're better, Uncle Josey," said he to the old man in the chimney- corner. "I caen't say I am," the other replied. "Well, Sir, I ded all 'zackly same like you tould me," said An Mary, "an maade the waater strong enow, an' stuffed the crock so full of 'brooms' as you may see et there 'pon the hurth thes mennet."

The gentleman, looking into the pot, said, "But what you have here isn't broom, it's heath!"

"Why, bless the man," said the old dame, getting vexed, "'tes grane griglans to the crock same what every-body do belong to maake brooms weth!—What else cud ee main?" After he had fully described the plant he meant, "Bless my sawl," said An Mary, "Why that what you're tellen me 'bout, weth the grane stimses an' all a flowers like furse-blowth up, es surely bannel! What out-o'-the-waay naames you up-country paiple do gev the thengs to be sure!" Bannel was procured, and with a decoction of that - and time - the old man got about again.

First published in "Stories and Folk-Lore of West Cornwall"

SOME CORNISH DIALECT NAMES FOR BIRDS

Apple-bird. Chaffinch (P)
Bud-picker. Bullfinch (P)
Burranet. Sheldrake (MAC)
Chaw. Chough (BEC)
Chickchacker. Wheatear (C)
Chickell. Wheatear (P)
Chiff Chaff. Chaffinch (MAC)
Chipper. Crossbill (MAC)
Chitty Wran. Common Wren (MAC)
Copper Finch. Chaffinch (MAC)
Dame-ku. Jack Snipe (RHB)
Dishwasher. Wagtail (U)
Elicomoanie. Tom-Tit (P)
Grey Bird. Song Thrush (MAC)
Hatter Flitter. Jack Snipe (MAC)
Hay Bird. Willow Wren (C)
Hoop. Bullfinch (MAC)
Horney Wink. Lapwing (C)
Kit. Red Kite (U)
Loon. Northern Diver (MAC)
Nope. Bullfinch (B)
Pedn-paly. Blue tit (MAC)

Peep-hawk. Kestral (U)
Peesweep. Lapwing (MAC)
Pope. Puffin (C)
Priden-Prall. Blue tit (MAC)
Rudbrist. Robin (U)
Stare. Starling (U)
Tinner. Water Wagtail (B)
Tom-Horry. Skua (U)
Vencock. Water Rail (U)
Wagel. Gull [Grey] (MAC)
Winnard. Redwing (P)
Woodwall. Woodpecker [Green]

Sources:

B = Bottrell (*Hearthside Stories*).
BEC = L. May Beckerlegge (*Old Cornwall*, Vol.VII, No. 10)
C = Thomas Quiller Couch of Bodmin (*Glossary of Cornish Dialect Words, East Cornwall*).
MAC = Margaret A Courtney of Penzance (*Glossary of Cornish Dialect Words, West Cornwall*).
P = Richard Polwhele
U = Unknown Source

-o-

DIALECT NONSENSE RHYME

"Joe Raw catched a craw'
Put un in a pasty,
Went to school, played the fool,
And said "Tes very nasty."

GRANDFUR'S TRIP TO TOWN

By E R Curtis

*(Awarded first prize and the Rosemergy Cup
in the 1980 Gorsedd Competition)*

Now I do knaw yew wud like to ear bout Grandfur going to Druth, et wus like this ere. Everybody do knaw Grandfur Trebilcock. Ee do live with Tom an Martha now, but ears ago et wus Grandfur's farm, till Tom an Martha got married an tucked over tha farm. Tha old people round do say that wen Grandfur was young ee used to say he wud marry a worker. Well ee ded that all right fur poor old Granny wus alus working. She ded tha milking, mated tha pigs an poultry. Wen tha houses comed to be clained out Grandfur add to go out en tha far field to look at the bullocks. Wen et was tailing time Granny dropped tha taties an plants an wen et comed to hoeing, there wus Granny agen. Grandfur used to say et maade un giddy ef ee done any hoeing. Aw but wen tha cheldern comed on to do a few jobs, Grandfer falled down an broke ees leg. Tha neighburs said ee wus running way from work. Anyway tha Doctor wanted to put un en Hospital but Grandfur maade so much fuss, deden want to go. En tha end tha Doctor said ee wud set ees leg there. Tha Doctor wus sum mazed an told Grandfur that tha beds en horsepital wus fur people who wus going to get better. That frightened Grandfur so much ee thought ee wus never going to get better no more, but ee ded ov course, but Grandfur never left tha farm for ears. Now a bit ago Martha went en Druth to buy a suit fur annaversary. She comed ome telling ow Druth was changed bra've. Now Grandfur wus alus contrairy like so ee sed any subbenhead wud knaw Druth. There wus bra yapping all round, een tha end Grandfur sed ee wud go en Druth an see fur hisself. Ee sed boy Jim can drive me in Tom's car but ee will ave to keep tha door open so I can jump out quick if I want too. Yeu are not lowed to drive like that sed Jim an nother thing, I caant drive cos I havven passed me test yet. Now go un do that to once sed Grandfur. It took Tom an Jim bra spur to explain to im how Jim cudden do that. En tha end et wus greed fur Tom to drive Grandfur an Jim to the village so they cud catch a bus. This was done on a Friday, fur Grandfur cudden go less twas market day. Wen the bus stopped fur em Grandfur told the conductor tha bus wadden made fitty.

The conductor axed wot wus wrong with et Grandfur sed there ought to be a door en tha back like a jingle so ee cud jump off ef anythin went wrong. The driver heered tha fuss an comed round to see wot twas all about en the end ee told Grandfur ee cud plaise isself ee cud ride en tha bus or walk. Grandfer thought a bit an en tha end got pon tha bus.

Now boy Jim put un next tha winder fur ee thought et may keep Grandfur quiet of ee looked out tha winder. Well they went on fur a bit then Grandfur saw Billy Scoble setting pon ees horse talking to sum men. Grandfur baled out stop the bus, stop the bus. Tha conductor comed running, wots tha matter ser ee sed.

Habben seed Billy Scoble fur ears sed Grandfur an I want ave bit chat with en. We caant stop tha bus like that we ave special places to stop sed tha conductor. Well that wus a special place fur me sed Grandfur, who wus mazed as a whitnick. Tha bus turned a corner an Billy Scoble wus out or sight. Grandfur wus still put out an glazed pon tha conductor an sed, wot do ee main calling me ser, ain't no ser, I'm Grandfur Trebilcock. Jim add sum job to quiet Grandfur down an by that time tha bus wus en Druth station. Jim got Grandfur off tha bus an comed down Station ill. Wots that riting pon tha road sed Grandfur. Jim told un that wus to say motor cars wus not allowed to go up the ill only come down. Ef I add a car sed Grandfur I wud drive un where I add a mind too. By then they add turned tha corner. Caant see no different ere sed Grandfur, town clock ees where et ave always bin, same as twas wen I wus young. I see they are shut up post office, cudden ford to run un spose wot with aving these ere motor vans an bykes all over tha place. Jim told un there ees a new post office up by Jack's Platt. Caant see ow they found room wot wuth tha raw ov houses and Balls shop an Snells bake ouse. Jim deden say nuthin fur ee knawed wot Grandfur wus fur saying wot ee thought. Jim sed ee want go bank furst an they got down be town clock. Et wus summer time an tha road wus full ov cars. Jim catched old ov Grandfur's arm an went cross tha road brave an speedy.

Wen they got tother side Grandfur axed Jim wot ee wanted to race cross like that fur. Jim sed ee deden want to be nacked down with they there cars. I shall walk cross as I mind too sed Grandfur an yew forgot me broked leg wen yew hailed me over ere deden ee. Jim wus fraid to leave Grandfur en tha street so took un en tha bank wuth un. Grandfur add a good look round, they must be doing good trade ere ee say's, they ave painted up brave since I wus en ere last. Jim done ees bisuness fast as ee could fur ee deden know wot Grandfur wus going to say. Jim held tha door open fur Grandfur to go out fust. Wen Grandfur was pon top tha steps ee seed a young woman comming up. Tha neck ov eer frock wus one ov they there low cut ones as they do call em. Grandfer looked down an wus struck speachless. Ee went down a couple ov steps an turned round. By this time she was on tha top step an boy Jim wus aving a good look at tha legs under tha mini skirt. All ov a sudden Grandfur baled out ay miss yew forgot to put yer frock on this morning. I ave not she sed this ere ees me dress. Then yew ought to be shamed oo yerself. I cud look right down to yer waist or nearly. Before ee cud say any more Jim jumped down tha steps an dragged Grandfur away an wus Jim's face red? Grandfur sputtered sum but soon cooled down. Now sed Jim we will buy a few things fur Mother. They went on a few steps, then Grandfur wanted to know were Tabbs Hotel wus, aw sed Jim et wus pulled down an this ere shop wus built. Wot they done that fur, said Grandfur, the gentry used to stay there. Come on sed Jim an went in tha shop ee picked up one ov they there wire baskets, Grandfur took one too, Jim told un to put et down as they wus to use fur people who wus going to buy things. Grandfur follered Jim gazing round pon all they shelves ov tins. Aw sed Grandfur after a bit lookee ere Jim they got tins ere wuth corn en em. Jim sed that wus sweet corn. Well sed Grandfur I ave seed bushels ov corn but never heared ov sweet corn afore, ef yew believe that yew will believe anything.

As twas Friday tha shop wus full ov people. After a bit Grandfur lost sight ov Jim, ee started to hollar. Boy Jim where are ee, where are ee. Ee cud be heared all over tha shop. Jim comed back an told un to stop hollaring. Jim deden knaw were to look an ees faace cud not be redder. I thought I add lost ee sed Grandfur.

Am going ketch hoald ov tha tale ov yeur jacket then I shaant be lost. I caant see they make much profit ere en this shop fur they are all elping theirself. Jim told un that people pay wen they git to the desk. After a spell they git out en tha street again. Now says Grandfur me feet are aching an I am starving hungard less go up Williams aiting ouse an ave bit dinner. Jim sed that shop wus shut up, caant be, not on a Friday, sed Grandfur. Ees tes, Jim told im we will go up Coffee Tavern fur sumthin to ate. Then Grandfur looked cross tha street. Who put that name over Trounsons shop ee sed. That shop now belong to Woolworths Jim sed. Well I shud think they wus mazed, they shops are common as can be fur I do hear there ees one in nearly every town sed Grandfur. Jim then took un up to Coffee Tavern. Jim axked Grandur wot ee wud like. Aw ee sed, a bit roast beef with taties, cabbage an mashed turmut. They doant serve that ere Jim sed an to save any more argement ee ordered fish chips an peas. Grandfur looked pon ees plaate sed never add fish en a jacket afore an et must ave took em a bra spur to cut tha taties up en jibs. Ee aite et all an Jim wus glad fur ee wus quiet wile ee wus aiting.

Now Jim wanted a pear ov boots but maade up ees mind ee wud sooner go barefoot than take Grandfur en nother shop, so wen they got outside ee maade fur tha station. Tha trip ome wus quiet fur Grandfur add a nap fur which Jim wus very thankful. Now Tom add greed to come to the village by five o'clock to pick em up but cos Jim add catched an earlier bus they add to wait fur Tom. After they got off tha bus Grandfur seed Liza Allen en er garden an went over to tell eer bout ees trip to town. Now Liza ees deef as a post an by tha time Grandfur add finished telling eer bout et, all tha village knawed wot add appened. After a bit Tom comed. Wen Jim got home ee told ees Mother ee wus never going to taake Grandfur to Druth again. Once wus nuff fur a life time. An who cud blame im.

First published in Old Cornwall, Vol. IX, No. 6.

-o-

DIALECT NONSENSE RHYME

Gurty Melk an' bearley bread no lack;
Pudden skins an a good shaip's chack;
A bussa of salt pelchers, 'nawther o' pork;
A good strong stummick, and a plenty o' work.

Edn' this good foe 'ee?

Madron Church.

SOME SAYINGS FROM OUR COMMUNITY
Madron

It's as blunt as a dag. It's as blunt as a miners axe.

Better fit I'd stayed 'ome. It would have been better if I had stayed at home.

Black as a turf rick toad. Said of something that was dirty.

S/he's carrying too much sail. Said of someone living beyond their means.

Don't know nuff to know they don't know nawthin. (Self explanatory).

Wot was a like? Raw milk me dear, raw milk. Referring to a first encounter after a row.

Comin' to come. Starting to work out; getting there when turning cream to butter

Full as a tick. Eaten too much.

Full of sauce and impertinence. Very Cheeky

Give un Bill tink. Give him a good hiding.

Hoity toity, I seen a white blackbird. Said by an old man who was trying to hold his own in a bragging competition. The white blackbird was a magpie.

I eats well and I sleeps well, but when it comes to work, I shivers all over.

It was laiken like a basket. Boat taking in water.

I've ate my words and I went no further. Fall silent

S/he looks like a bundle of straw tied in the middle. Said of someone who is overweight.

S/he has more mouth than teeth. S/he has to much to say.

S/he's some mussy toad. Grubby person and ways

It's time to go up tembern hill. Time for bed

You don't need that mor'n a toad needs side pockets. You don't need it.

Feelin some leary, you! Hungry - weak and faint from hunger

With thanks to Zip Roberts
and Members of the Madron Old Cornwall Society.

-o-

A PROPOSAL

Naw, my deear, I allus sed I'd never marry a widdaman, but I'll tell 'ee 'ow et comed about. When faather died, ould Squire wanted th' 'ouse fur th' new gaame-keeper, so I tooked they two lil' rooms in behind Maary Dawe, where Jane Penberthy d' live now. They be two poky lil' rooms, sure 'nuff—I cud'n git me thengs in! So I ax'd Jem Walters ('e'd ben a wedda-man 'bout two 'eears then) ef 'e knawed anybody ded want t' buy a chess-en-drores: I tho't 'e'd be s' likely knaw es anybody, bein' en th' carpentry traade. Jem dedn' seem knaw nawbody, but a'ter a bit 'e sed, "Semmen t' me, Maary, thee's better breng thy few thengs long t' my 'ouse, an com'st long weth 'em."

I dedn' say nawthen then; I was bit took 'back, es you med say.

Nex' Sunday ebenen, Jem was waitin' fur me, down the laane, a'ter Chapel, so I up an' axed un, "Dost mane wot thee's sed, Jem, laast Friday?" "Iss, ef thee 'rt wellen, Maary," 'e sed.

"Wull," I sed, "I ben thenken 'pon et, an—b'lieve I wull; I cudn't 'ford peart wi' Mawther's ould chess-en-drores, a'ter all."—Aw, me deear! A wumman was waanted en thet 'ouse bad nuff, I c'n tell 'ee! A man's a wisht pore theng t'lev by hisself.

E. A. L.

First published in Old Cornwall, Vol.I, No.4.

CHOIR OWTEN

by "Penwith" (Mrs. James)

(Awarded first prize in the dialect verse section at the 1925 Gorsedd)

Good Fridai wuz a crisp, cleer, dai,
Wen all the town ded 'omaige pay,
To ainshent church wid staiple tall,
Standin' near the 'arbour wall.

But medst the gloom a light ded shine,
Fer thai from sai an' from the mine,
A 'oliday wuz en the air,
A trip to Zennor Churchtown feer.

Choir owten cum but wonce a yeer,
Bringin' goodwill an' joy an' cheer,
As lads an' lassies, men an' boys,
Forsook theer tools, forsook theer toys.

An' set out on a merry spree,
Across the moors, towards the sai,
The rugg'd moors, wid yalla gorse,
An' thrift, bracken, an' bramble coarse.

Fer ev'ry Jan es Jaine ded malt,
As thai went traipsin' thru' the strait,
Up to Rosewall an' Zennor wheer
Thai'd find a farm wid welcum cheer.

Fer Farmer Osborne's wife ded maike,
The rechest craim, an' breer rech caike,
So to es farm thai maide theer wai,
Thai lads an' lassies en that day.

Sum walk'd, sum ran, sum took theer time,
Sum rest'd neath an ainshent sign,
Pointin' the wai to 'amlet small,
Which rest'd on a Cornish wall.

The sky wuz blue, the air wuz chill,
The lettel 'amlet nestl'd still,
Around the ainshent churchtown theer,
Sum 'ansum sight I do decleer.

An' en the Church the Choir ded walk,
Thai paused a while, an' ded not talk,
An' look'd upon the Mermaaid feer,
Wid feshes taail an' golden heer.

Fer centuries shai'd watch'd the crowd,
Admire 'er silent, or aloud,
But nivver wonce 'er taaile 'ad tawld,
O' bygone dais en yeers o' awld.

Thin from the Church thai maaide theer way,
To Farmer Osborne's en that dai,
To rest theer weary souls a while,
An' pause to kewse, an' laugh, an' smile.

'Cos, wonce the Osborne's farm wuz sain,
Won thaut o' saffern caike an' craim,
An' 'hevva' caike, an' fairins swait,
An' 'ome cured 'am, an' aiven mait !

An' a desh of tai, strong an' swait,
To aise the burden of the fait;
'Cos five 'ole miles thai'd traips'd that dai,
An' now 'ad cum the time fer plai.

A time to ait, a time to drenk,
A time to cogitaite an' thenk,
About the five miles back to town,
To ainshent village o' renown.

The Choir stell 'ad a task that dai,
An' as thai paus'd from work an' plai,
Theer minds wid music thai ded fill,
Music fer sai, an' moor, an' 'ill.

Haydn's "Creashun" fill'd the air,
As thai rehears'd en farmyard bare,
The organist ded waive es 'and,
An' bass, an' alto, 'ee bid stand.

'Osses an' cows en wonder stood,
En farmyard an' en stalls of wood,
As Haydn's music fill'd the air,
That Aister time en Zennor feer.

Refresh'd en body, an' en soul,
The Choir as won an' as a 'ole,
Ded bid ferwell to farm 'awse theer,
En Zennor Churchtown, awld an' reer.

An 'omeward thai set out agin,
The boys an' girls, wemmen, an' men,
All raidy fer theer concert night,
Et railly wuz a merry sight.

That aivenen en Chapel 'igh,
Haydn's "Creashun" raich'd the sky,
As the Choir sung to young an' awld,
An Aister message ded unfawld.

Et spawk o' 'ope an' comfort, too,
To paiple of lands awld an' new;
o' lastin' paice fer all the world,
United, wid banners unfurl'd.

An' as night drew across the sky,
The Choir re-lived wid many a sigh,
Ets 'appy owten en that dai,
A dai wen music 'ad ets wai.

First published in Old Cornwall, Vol. VIII, No. 7.

-o-

SOME SAYINGS FROM OUR COMMUNITY

Newlyn

A 'ead like a bladder o' lard. Said of a Bald man.

A hatful of wind. No real wind at all.

Ain't seen 'air nor 'ide ov'en. He/s is lying low.

Face like a rusticock. Red faced.

Feedin' yer face. Eating.

Goin' like clappers ov a mill. Rushing about.

If s/he cain't drive they waint ride. Must be top dog.

Keepin' out the road. Ashamed.

Like Great Aunt Jane, don't want nobody with 'er and don't want to be left alone.

Nawthen' going nowhere and less comin' home.

Not very onions. Unfriendly.

Proper bojock (Bawjack). Rough, Uncouth.

S/he d'know everything' about everythin' an' a lot more besides.

S/he 'ave got to be 'ead an' chief.

S/he's mouth out. All talk but nothin else.

S/he's some mussy toad. Said of a messy person.

Stop hollerin' and ollerin' an' kickin' up a carousel (pronounced karowsal). Be Quiet.

Sun crackin' the 'edges. Very hot day.

Wot a life says Alfick, gi'us a chaw (of tobacco). Fed up but resigned.

With thanks to Zip Roberts, Audrey Thomas and Sandra Vingoe.

-o-

TROON CHARACTERS

Old "Marget" R— used to go round selling griglan besom, which she made from heather collected on a croft near her house, not far from Troon.

She would often carry them down to Dolcoath mine. Sometimes she would meet "Capun Josiah," who would say to her: "Marget," he would say, "Didn't I tell 'ee not to bring no more brooms till after next count." "Why, perhaps so, Capun 'Sigh, but, theer, I had them by me, and I said to myself—'What's a bur'n of brooms to a great Bal like this?'"

She lived in a small cottage of three rooms—thatched—and had more than a dozen children. One of these, named "Sampy," died not so many years since in Grass Valley, Montana, a rich man. In their young days they were very poor, however, and old "Marget," besides her brooms, had only three little quillets of ground on which she kept a "little cow" for her support.

One time a man tried to take these away from her. "Marget" was much upset, and eventually went into Redruth to see Mr. "Lanjohn" [Lanyon]. "I tell 'ee," she said, "the old broom edn't wore out yet!" [here making a sign like a broom going round on a tin-stream], "nor the old broomer idn't finish d yet, neither" [shaking the money in the pocket of her skirt], "but, all the same, Mr. Lanjohn, that fella's nothen moore than a black-faaced ould divil!"

She was short, thick-set, and very stout.

First Published in Old Cornwall, Vol.I, No.6.

-o-

SHOPPING IN LUNNON CHURCH-TOWN

Good evening' Miss Eddy, I'm glad 'e 'ave come so now I can push to make tay; t'others are inside so take off 'e cloak an' if 'e plase you may tend to the tray.

Now I tell 'e what I seen down Lunnon Church-Town where housen do reach to the sky an' the paple are nothin' but imperin' tread, I cunna abide 'em, not I. I goad to a smart shop down Prince Regent Street an' marcy how shamed I did feel, for the tenders were men all dressed up so fine an' lookin' so genteel. I goes up to one an' I say's, "Now look 'e 'eer, I want a new gown, so take down a gingham or cotton or stuff which never is worn in this town." "We are silk mercers, madam, and only sell silk" said this danderfied know-nothin' fop. I said to 'im, "Why, down in Cornwall they do sell all sorts, so yourne can't be much of a shop."

First published in Old Cornwall, Vol. VI, No.12.

-o-

SOME SAYINGS FROM OUR COMMUNITY

Cury on the Lizard

As heavy as a witch, four score and ten.

As hardened as Pharoah. Said of someone who is being stubborn.

A crowing hen and a whistling woman are no good to anyone. To hear a hen attempt to crow as I have is weird beyond belief.

Eat the herring off a grid iron. Said by someone who is very hungry.

Face like a rubber horse. Said of a a brazen-faced person.

Greyer than the guts of a toad. Something that is dark, dull and sinister.

Found a gold mine, 'ave 'ee? Remark to someone who suddenly appears to have money to spare.

He was grinning like a chad. A chad is a fish with a large mouth.

Stank on they emmetts, Boy! Kill the ants.

He's been as sick as a shag. This sea bird regurgitates its food to its young, so the origin is there, and applies to those vomiting.

S/he's scrumped up I like a shay wheel! Shoulders withdrawn and bent and rounded as if suffering from the cold. Withdrawn and miserable. Relates to animals or human beings.

I'm hotter than hell with the door shut.

Thanks to Danny Green of Redruth Old Cornwall Society.

-o-

JINNY PENHAUL

by Molly Bartlett

Has't tha ever tho't thee'st been bewitched,
When everything went awry!
When th' children ailed, an th' crops all failed,
An' thee watched th' ol' cow die?

When I was a cheel, down 'ere in Penvose
Some 'nation queer things come to pass,
An' ol Jinny Penhaul was blamed for 'em all;
An' t'was sed that she went to Black Mass!

Well, when I was 'bout seben 'ear old,
I minchied from skule one 'ot day.
I knowed it was wrong, an' th' day was so long,
Wi' nobody else there to play.

I e't up me crowst, an' me pasty too,
An' was lairey's a 'ound when Church clock struck two,
When 'long comes ol' Jinny, pickin' sticks in 'er pinny,
An' she gi'ed me a rare taalkin' to!

She thre'tened to take me straight 'ome to me Ma,
An' I very soon wished that she 'ad,
For she put me to work like a very ol Turk,
Tho' I tould 'er I veeled very bad.

I carried 'er fardel, t'was 'eavy as lead,
An' she kept pilin' more on th' top.
I begged 'er for mercy, an' she thre'tened to curse me,
An' she poked me behind if I stopt!

When we got to 'er 'ouse, way down Deepy lane,
Wi' no other dwellin' in sight
She shoved 'broad th' door, an' there 'pon th' floor
Sat a thumpin' gurt toad, black as night!

I scritched like a witneck, an' faaled to me knees,
Me chimmy stuck fast to me back,
I started to cry an' 'e spit in my eye,
An blowed up til' I tho't 'e would crack!

I tried to run off, but ol' Jinny catched me,
"There's a passel o' chores thee mus' do,
Take thikky paddick an' fill it, an' weed out me quillet,
An' skin they there rabburts for stew.

I weeded 'er quillet, as best as I could,
But shee kicked up a bra' how de-do,
Cos I pulled up 'er yarrow, an' ruined 'er marrow,
An' vooched on 'er stinkin' ol' rue.

She gi'ed me th' paddick to fetch 'er some waater,
My soul, t'was a clumsy gurt thing.
When I got to th' peath I was 'frighted to death,
For toads sot all round in a ring!

I let go th' paddick an' scat'n to sherds,
An' I took to me 'eels like th' wind,
'Ard coosed by black cats, an' black birds like gurt bats,
An' toads jumpin' like hosses behind!

I faaled down in a 'eap when I got to our door,
An' poor Mawther tho't I was daid.
When I tould 'er 'bout Jinny, she put 'er haid in 'er pinny,
An' called me a bad, wicked maid.

First published in "Cornish Dialect"
Federation of Old Cornwall Societies, 1982.

-o-

DIALECT WORDS FROM OUR COMMUNITY

Pentewan

Chirky Wheeler. Cake mixture which is fried like a pancake.

Clopper. Lame.

Cold Lauch. Cold and unappetizing food.

Dippie. Rancid, mouldy (usually food).

Flink. To shake water off ones hands with abrupt movement.

Geeking & Gunning. To stare fixedly (Gunning is allied to short-sightedness).

Glancing. Travelling at fast speeds (almost reckless).

Heaving. Busy as in the Main street of a town with many people.

Ikey. Person who thinks s/he's a cut above the rest.

Riffles. Fallen slates after a gale.

Sky-Blue. Milk, flour and water boiled.

Stuggy. Stocky, thick-set.

Thirl. Thin, lean.

Thanks to Mrs C.A. Stark, Recorder Pentewan Old Cornwall Society

SOME CORNISH SHIBBOLETHS.

Floating about in Cornwall are some curious sayings or sentences in which as many local words as possible have been crammed together. There are always many variants of these; and naturally enough, since they are passed on from one person to another, continually losing or gaining something in the process. Two short ones are known to almost everyone: -

'Ded 'ee ever see a mollard clunk a gay?' Did you ever see a drake swallow a sherd of china-ware?' Some times the mollard is 'down in a cundard' and 'clunking gays, shards, and hellins.'

'There's a muryan on thy nuddick' is another equally well-known. 'There's an ant on the back of thy neck.' Such sentences are often used as tests of the Cornishness of anyone claiming to belong to our ancient race, and though they are mainly dialect English, 'clunk' and 'muryan' at least belong to our old Celtic language.

Here is a longer one:- **'There was a man putting hellin-stones 'pon the paint-'ouse out in the bully-court, and he fall'd down on to the caunse and scat his nuddick so he caan't clunky.'** 'There was a man putting slates on the pent-house out in the pebbled court yard, and he fell down on to the paving and hit the back of his neck so that he can't swallow.'

There are, I daresay, a dozen versions of this, most of them shorter than the above; but still longer is one called 'The Cloam Man,' which is almost a story:

'As I was going uplong t'other day, I seed a cloam-man with a flasket o' cloam 'pon a's head. A knacked a's foot 'gin the durns o' the dooer; faalled down 'pon the caunse; tored a's flasket en lembs; scat a's cloam all to sherds, and put a's nuddick out of truckle, so's he cudn' clunky. Up comes a's missus en some stroath. – 'Lor'-a-miny!' sez she 'Here's our Jan, down en a quaame! Edn' a fine an' wisht, you?'

Here we have no more Celtic words than in the shorter version, unless 'stroath' is one; but a saying, variously reported, though in words always much as follows, is quoted as having been given as evidence by a Sennen fisherman at a Board of Trade Shipwreck inquiry held in London, and this gives us two more:

'Well, gintlemen, you've broft me all the way heere uplong for to tell 'ee what I do knaw 'bout this 'eere wreck! All I can tell 'ee es, the shep come en 'pon the Cowloe, an' scat all to scubmow, an' the browjans was all about the cove an' washin' up 'pon our caunse!

Scat to scubmow, 'broken to chips,' and 'browjans,' bits, are very near to Cornish *scatties dho scubmow* and *browjion*, and might stand more chance of being understood in Brittany than in London. This last is reported as a genuine speech, and is a very likely one from such a man on such a subject; the others, too, are probably merely improved versions of something once actually heard. The temptation to put in another word to increase the 'local colour' is difficult to resist, and many readers will be annoyed, perhaps, to find that their own, the 'only correct' versions of these sayings are not given. They should report these to the recorders of their own O.C.S., together with any other such randigals as they may have heard.

Robert Morton Nance

First published in Old Cornwall, Vol. I, No. 1.

-o-

DRAA' FOO'TH AND BREAD YOUR BAASINS!

At Feastentide gatherings in West Cornwall this was always the call that invited guests, assembled from all the parishes round, to draw forth their chairs to the table, and prepare for the first course of the "Faisten Denner." A cloamen basin was set before each guest and into this he was expected to crumble his slice off the nutty "kettle loaf" before the "Faisten brath" was poured into it. A later refinement was to cut up the bread and set "breaded" basins at each place, when '"Draa' foo'th!" alone would be the invitation given. The broth at such festival dinners was the liquor of the meat-and-vegetable course, these having been cooked with the dumplings, all in the same great crock set on the brandis over the open-hearth fire of furze and turf.

As an invitation to guests at "Cornish Dinners" this hearty welcome to table might well be revived. It would at least suggest time genial atmosphere of Old Cornwall.

First published in Old Cornwall, Vol. I, No. 2.

A DIALECT ALPHABET

By Ken Phillipps

Aglets are berries on a hawthorn tree bough.
Bottoms are valleys untouched by the plough.
Crib's a mid-morning snack, going down good.
Durn is a door-frame that's made out of wood.
Evil's a fork, for spreading out dung.
Fermaigue's to deceive, by act or by tongue.
Gaddling means drinking as fast as you can.
A *hobbledehoy* is between boy and man.
Iles are the beards that on barley are seen.
Jig means a mockery of God or the Queen.
Keeve is a big tub for salting a pig.
Things 'teared all to *lerrups*' are not very big.
A *mincher* is one who escapes out of school.
A *new vang* is new, but won't last as a rule.
Ovees is a word for the eaves of a roof.
Paddick's a small pitcher' not breakage-proof.
Q is a *quailaway*, a stye on the eye.
River is any small stream that runs by.
There are two words for 'scratch', to sclum and to *sclow*.
T is a *touch-pipe* – 'Let's have a smoke now'.
Ugly describes your bad temper, not looks.
Veer is a farrow; one that still sucks.
W is *wisht* when things badly are done.
X is for *zackly* without the 'x' on.
Y is for *yorks* to keep trouser legs clean.
Z for *zam-zoodled*, half-baked, poor cuisine.
There are twenty-six letters in dialect too.
Here's a number of words that are Cornish for you.

First published in Old Cornwall, Vol. 11, No. 6.

BILLY TELLING THE NEWS TO YOUNG FARMER KESSELL (A Parody)

"Hullaw Billy! How be'ee? How es oal home?"
"Bad, shore nuff. T'howl magpie es dade."
"Aw! Ee's dade, es a? How cum that te be?"
"Ded a? What waz et a ait?"
"Hoss-flesh, tell a cudd'n clunk no moar."
"How cum a te git that sort un mait?"
"Maister's hosses."
"Thay baen't dade be'um?"
"Iss, oal awin te haard work."
"What haard work do'ee main?"
"Thay putt'em te draa waater."
"What vur?"
"Te put tha vire out weth."
"Vire! What vire?"
"Doant'ee knaw; Way Maister's houz es oal a burn down."
"Vaather's houz a burn down! How waz et?"
"That gashly owld lanterns ded et, I de theenk."
"Lanturns! What be'ee taalkin abaout? Whane waz et?"
"That there time whane we was berrin yewer poar mawther."
"Mawther! Es she dade?"
"Iss, and nevvur spok no moar aafter thaht."
"Aafter what?"
"Aafter ower owld maister dide."
"Es vaather dade too?"
"Iss, a tuk to es bade direckly a waz towld."
"Towld! What waz a towld?"
"Desmal newas, plais shore."
"Aw loar! What wisht newas waz et?"
"Wale ef yew must knaw I'le tell'ee, tha Bank's a brok.!
"Aw dear! Aw dear! Thickky es tha wishtest theeng un oal. We shul oal be scat, every wawn un us."

Dialect use illustrated by F W P Jago in his 1882 publication "The ancient language and the dialect of Cornwall.."
Published in Old Cornwall, Vol 12, No. 2.

SOME CORNISH DIALECT SMUGGLING TERMS

Anker. Small cask of handy size used by smugglers for carrying by hand or on horse back.

Bolt. Place where smuggled goods were hidden. This could take the form of a well, hole in a Cornish hedge or a tunnel or cave. In fact anywhere that was felt to be away from prying eyes.

Breachy (bree'chi). Applied to smuggled goods that have been impregnated with salt water.

Creeper. Iron bar with multi hooked end. Tied to a rope and draggen along the seabed to hook up the ankers which had been sunk to hide them. Source: Short

Custom (pronounced Coostem). Raw smuggled spirits "A drap of Coostem".

Dollop. A packet or lump of tea, weighing from 6 to 18lbs, so packed for the convenience of smuggling. Source: Courtney

Kiddliwink. Name for a beerhouse. The name came about because smuggled brandy was kept in a Kiddle (Kettle) and when a customer wanted some he would wink at the Kiddle. Source: *Cornishman* newspaper, Nov. 17 1881.

Kimbly. A gift given to the first person to bring news that the boat (smugglers) had arrived.

Moonshine. Spirit that has been smuggled.

Smacksman. The name given to the person who determines the precise spot on the coast where a cargoe was to be landed.

Sampson. A drink of cider, brandy with a little water and sugar.

Trade. Smuggled Goods.

Troacher. A hawker of smuggled goods.

Tubs. Larger form of anker

From the Editor's Collection.

-o-

"TURNIN' TH' TAABLES"

by D.E.M. Trenberth

Faather' 'anged up 'is cep and crib bag, an' taaked off 'is boots in th' back kitchen, then padded inta th' kitchen t' put 'is slippers on what I'd got warmin fur un in fore a roarin' fire. .'E'd warmed 'is 'ands, announced "Tiz good t' see a fire maid, 'tiz raw out", an' 'ad turned roun' t' warm 'is beer back, 'fore 'e nawticed th' carrycot in th' corner.

"Aw ", 'e grawned "Wha's th' row 'bout this time"?

"Sh', she'll 'ear 'ee." I warned.

"I dun't caare." Faather said, but 'e law'rd 'is voice 'Wha's th' matter with 'er aany'ow? She awnly been marrade two 'ears, an' this be th' third time she've left Roger. I thawt now she got th' baaby, she'd 'ave grawed up a bit. Bawth uv urn should 'ave more sense.

"SHE" was Jean, our daughter, an' my reacshun 'ad bane 'zackly th' saame as Faather's, when I'd sane 'er get out uv th' 'ire car after dinner. 'An in caase you be thinkin' we be unnacheral parents, I 'aasten t' explaan that we by oways glad t' see she an' Roger when they come, but not when she d' come on 'er awn, 'cause she've "lef' un". P'raps we'd spoil'd 'er a bit, well I knaw Faather 'ad, but like 'e, I was beginnin' t' think she shouln' come runnin' 'ome t' we ev'ry time they 'ad a row. They'd bin marrade awnly six months when they 'ad th' fust one. 'E'd bin unwise enough t'critacise 'er cookin', an' she'd flaared up an' told un 'e could do 'is awn, an' she 'awped as 'twud poisun un, if it didn' chuck un fust. 'Ome she'd come t' we, (they awnly lived 'bout thirty miles 'way) squallin', an' "She'd lef' un fur good. If 'e ringed she didn' want t' spake to un".

She mawped about fur thray days, then 'e ringed an' said if she'd got awver 'er bad temper, t' come 'ome, all was fergived. I taaked th' message, an' passed it on. More tears an' recriminations!

Roger 'ad come at th' wake end. They was in th' front room fur a bit, then comed out all sheepish an' said they'd maade it up. Our relafe was shortlived. Five months laater she was back agen.

She was 'expectin' be now, an' 'e'd bin tackless 'nough t' tell 'er th' plaace was like Lancin' Jail. Spawse she 'adn' bn falin' well, an' 'adn' tidied up. Well I was a bit symputhetic then, men be'nt oways very understandin'. 'E awnly waited fawr days that time 'fore 'e fetched 'er. It did'n same t' affect they much, but me an' Faather was nervous wrecks after th' visits.

Well this time she stayed a fortnight. I reckun 'e was glad t' catch up on slape 'fore 'e fetched 'em.

We sit down an' 'ad a 'ot cup a tay when we'd waaved 'em off, then Faather said,

"I can't put up wi' no more maid. You'll 'ave t'think uy somethin'."

"'Ow bout you? 'Ebm you got no ideas?" I ask, but Father 'ad t' admit 'e was beat.

Well, I addled me brains awver th' nex' few wakes, then suddenly I got it 'Twas s' simple, I dun't knaw 'ow I 'adden thawt uv it afore. Me chance t' tell Faather comed when 'e'd sit down t' tay, an said, "Yur maid, this mate be a bit tough, idden it?"

"Tha's it," I holla'd, "Tha's all you c'n do, find fault." Faather was staarin' like a stat. 'Ere, 'old on maid, I awnly said——"

"I knaw what you said," I brawk in. Well, you can coo yur awn food t'morra. I be goyn."

"Goyn? Goyn where?" Faather gasp'd.

"I'm lavin' 'ee, tha's what," I told un "Of all th' thawtless, selfish——" I 'ad t' stop as Faather's mouthful uv tay 'e'd clunked, 'ad gone down th' wrong way, an' I 'ad t' thump un on th' back. Then I bust out laughin' at th' expreshun on 'is faace.

"I reckun you be proper maazed" Faather said.

"No I be'nt," I told un I got th' answer t' our problem wi' Jean. Wha's sauce fur th' goose——So I be goyn t' stay wi' she an' Roger. Yur ears'll be burnin mind, an' when you ring up after thray days, I shan't spake to 'ee, so there."

Be this time Faather'd got th' idea, an' joined in th' laughin'.

"Yur maid, do "ee think 'twill work"?

"You bet 'twill, I said, "You'll see, Roger'll bring me back on th' Sunday if you ring. Get un t' talk some sense inta me."

Well off I went t' Jeans nex' mornin', 'avin left 'nough food t' kape Faather fur wakes.

"Er faace, when she awpened 'er door was a picshur an' 'er "Mam, you can't mane you've left Dad", when I'd sqeezed out a few tear (Yur I reckun I've missed me vawcaation. That Sarah Bern'ardt couldn' 'ave old a candle t'me.) an' told me taale uv woe.

I said "I'd bin tempted t' lave un 'eaps uv times, but stayed out uv 'abit.

But she'd shawed me 'ow silly an' spineless I was. If she could lave Roger I could lave Dad. I didn' want t' be no burden to 'em, an' I'd pay me way. If I could stay a few wakes while I got me bearin's, I'd look out fur a li'l job.

'Twas grand t' think I 'ad she t' turn to— —"And so on and so forth. I was miser'ble" all afternoon, an' grumbled 'bout Faather (all on th' lines of she, when she come t' we.)

I faled a bit mean when she said they'd 'ave t' move th' baaby's cot inta th' boxroom. I'd 'ave liked th' dear uv un in wi' me, but no, that wouldn' be th' way t' bring up modern baabiesl

When Roger come 'ome, she taaked un in t' th' front room, an' I spawse explaaned it all. 'E come inta th' kitchen all 'eat-ty, an' said 'e 'spected 'twould all blaw awver. But 'e was s' puzzled as she was, I knaw. Th' nex' few days I must 'ave bin a sore trial fur Jean. Under 'er fate all th' time. I never realis'd 'ow 'ard 'twas t' be mis'rable.

Things went accordin' t' plan. I wouldn' spake t' Faather when 'e ringed (but I wrawt a long letter an' snaked out t' pawst it). When they tried t' spake bout Faather, I'd rant on bout un, ur squall an' 'ave t' run out uv th' room. Th' poor sawls didn' 'ave a minute t' theirselves an' I reckun they was gettin' desp'rut be th' time Faather 'phawned on th' Sunday.

Sure 'nough, Roger called me in t' th' frontroom an' I was "persuaaded" t' go 'ome an' try agen. 'E would run me 'ome after dinner. I thanked 'em fur 'avin me, an' said I 'oped 'twould work out, but if it didn' I knawed I'd be s' welcome with they as Jean'd be with me, nex' time she comed.

"Ess well, er," Roger cough'd, "Me an' Jean 'ave bin thinkin', an we reckun 'tis time we weather'd our awn storms, so t' spake. There's bound t' be lots uv ups an' downs, but we mus' manage be ourselves. 'Tisn' fair t' burden you an' Dad all th' time."

"P'raps you be right Roger" I said, all meek "I'll 'ave t' tell Faather that."

Well 'e dropped me t' th' gaate. I was glad 'e didn' come in. I didn' want un t' see 'ow plased I was t' see Faather agen, an' I'm sure Faather couldn' 'ave acted no diffurnt t' saave 'is life.

Well that was a year ago, an' we eb'm 'ad no more surprise visits, though they've spent wake ends an' a 'oliday with us. So I reckun my shock tactics done th' trick.

Now if you d' get aany matrimawnial problems, you knaw who t' contac' dun't 'ee?

First published in "Cornish Dialect" Federation of Old Cornwall Societies 1982

OLE BOOD

(From an incident at Waterloo Station)

I went to London and Mother too.
Us zeed the Thames. the Tower, the Zoo,
Us did'n knaw then what more ver do,
So us traapsed away to Waterloo
Ver home to Bood.

Our 'eads was addled with sights and sounds
Our 'earts was sick and tired of towns,
Our veet was achin' ver Zummerleaze Downs
In dear ole Bood.

There was crowds of volks in the Bookin' 'all,
But of volks us knawed there wad'n a sawl
So I sticked me 'ead in a pigeon awl -
'Two tickets ver Bood.'

I looked to Mother, 'er face was red,
'Hush Jan, be maazed? 'tis Bude,' 'er said,
But then the Clerk 'ee shawed 'es 'ead,
And - 'Good Old Bood!'

All eager-like I says to 'un
'Be you from Bood, then, too, my son?'
'Ees, father, fey I be—no fun,
I be from Bood.'

'And up ta "Street" where I was born
Could yer the sea and the coachman's horn,
And I tell 'ee London's cruel forlorn
Beside ole Bood.'

'I wad'n a-born ta Bood' says I,
But Bood I live and there I'll die,
'Tis a place where a-body can see the sky
Is dear ole Bood.'

'And the streets by clayn and the houses too,
And the Station beateth Waterloo,
And even poor volks gets a voo,
Home there to Bood.'

'So, sonny, I'll see ole Rood to day,
And the Ceres sailin' in the Bay
And the beautiful sunset o'er the zay,
And when I sees yer volks I'll say
Yer love to Bood.'

Provided by Audrey E. Aylmer Bude and Stratton District O.C.S.

-o-

SOME DIALECT WORDS FROM OUR COMMUNITY

Bude and Stratton.

Addle Egg. Non-fertile egg under sitting hen.
'Ammertinker (vb). To 'fiddle' about, achieving very little.
Arrish Moo. Small round temporary rick for drying sheaves.
Airey Mouse. Hairy mouse or bat.
Blacklade. 'Blacking' for polishing kitchen range.
Blownk. Burning, flying ember.
Bodley. Cast-iron cooking range.

Cricket. Three-legged milking stool.

Dewsnell. Slug.

Doaney. Damp with dew.

Dreckly. Presently... after unspecified time lag.

Drogg (vb). To stop motion of a machine.

Enjus Gurt. Superlative of big or large sized.

Figgitydick. Pudding containing currants.

Floppy-dop. Foxglove.

Gambades. Big, awkward feet in animal or man.

Nattlin-Grace. Axle-grease from melted-down intestines.

Provided by members of Bude and Stratton District O.C.S.

-o-

Good Auld Pasty

Some doant like pasty, so they say
But I asks 'em 'ave they tried
The rale thing, like we folks ate,
Well made, well baked; not dried
The rale thing ez full an plump.
Bulged by the trade inside,
With gravy oosin from the leaks an mate,
Till nearly swemmin on yer plate.
But take a tip from one oo knaws
Ef you want 'un to dejest;
Ee never must sam soddled be,
Or you woan't get 'um off yer chest.

From Sandra Vingoe's postcard collection

www.ingramcontent.com/pod-product-compliance
Lightning Source LLC
Chambersburg PA
CBHW031432040426
42444CB00006B/777